Le Corbusier
Monastery of Sainte-Marie de La Tourette
1953-60

ル・コルビュジェ
ラ・トゥーレット修道院
1953-60

Paper Relief of the Modulor

Le Corbusier
Monastery of Sainte-Marie de La Tourette

Photos: Kazuyoshi Miyamoto　Text: Jin Kurita

目　次

◇修道院写真	4-11,16-37
◇図面、ディテール	12-15,38
◇修道院の原点を強く意識した巨匠の円熟期の大冒険	
修道院の立地	40
建築的主張の発展形	40
ラ・トゥーレット修道院の座標	42
技法のブラッシュアップ	44
デザインソースは日本建築？	44
傑出したプロデューサー	46
音楽家で構造家でもあるクセナキス	48
居心地のよい修道僧の個室	50
◇「修道院」像の大いなる振幅	52

Contents

◇Photos of the Monastery	4-11,16-37
◇Plans of the Monastery, Detail	12-15,38
◇Strong Awareness to the Origins of a Monastery	
Odyssey of Master Architect in His Mature Age	
Location of the Monastery	41
Development of Architectural Assertion	41
Positioning the Monastery of La Tourette	43
Brushup of Techniques	45
Japanese Architecture as Design Sources?	45
Outstanding Producer	47
Xenakis as a Musician and Structural Engineer	49
Cozy Cells for Monks	51

▲ 南西外観。ハーモニカ状の開口は修行僧と教師の僧房（4、5階）。その下は教室の並ぶ階（3階）と食堂（2階）で、1/fゆらぎ風配置のランダムなマリオンが強烈な印象を与える。

Southwest appearance. Harmonica-looking openings are cells for monks and teachers (3rd and 4th floors). Underneath are classrooms (2nd floor) and a refectory (dining hall) (1st floor) and the mullions pitched randomly like 1/f fluctuation give a deep impression.

◀ 西面外観。3階は入口階、上の2層は階高がおさえられている。2、3階の波動リズムガラス面(オンデュラトワール)の存在感が圧倒的。

West appearance. The entrance is located on the 2nd floor. The floor-to-floor distance of the upper two levels is short. The undulatory-rhythm glass walls (ondulatoire) of the 1st and 2nd floors have a dominant presence.

▲ レセプション奥に位置するベンチ。重厚だが質素な外観からピロティをくぐり、様々な形態が混在している中庭が一望できる演出。

Bench behind the reception. After you go through the pilotis from the solemn and simple outside, a means to give a sweeping view of the garden court where various shapes are mixed will be available to you.

◀ 右手の大壁面は聖堂の壁、その下は、聖堂の聖具室部分に光を落とす「軽機関銃の天窓」。開口部は夏至の太陽の軌道に向けられている。コンクリート屋根に張られた芝が無機質な中庭に生命感を与えている。

The wall on the right side is one of the holy shrine. Beneath is "mitraillettes" (machine gun of light), which cast light on the sacrarium of the holy shrine. The opening is focused towards the orbit of the solstitial sun. Lawn grasses on the concrete roof give a feeling of vitality to the harsh garden court.

▶ 閲覧室内部からの景色。手前は4階の通路にいたる階段だが、現在は使用されていない。

View from the reference room. Foreground is the stairway to the 3rd floor, but it is unused now.

▲ 修道院の東側ファサード。右に聖堂、左に修道院のエントランスとその上部2層が修道士の僧房階。マッシブな聖堂と、コの字型の僧房棟の「付かず離れず」の間合いが絶妙。

East façade of the Monastery. The holy shrine on the right side and the entrance of the Monastery with two layers of monk cells on top of it are on the left. Superb is putting it mildly to describe the difference between the massive holy shrine and the U-shape monk cell wing.

▶ 西日に浮かぶ聖堂。撮影時は夏至に近い6月。太陽はこの時期、真西より北側に沈む。撮影時刻は午後8時頃。
台形の壁の上に大きく跳ね出す鐘楼が最も劇的に見えるアングル。

Holy shrine in the sunset. Taken in June, near the midsummer. The sun is setting in the northern side from the west. Shooting time was about 8pm.
The bell tower, hanging over the trapezial wall, looks most dramatic from this angle.

8

修道院の東側ファサード。マッシブな下階に僧房階が乗る。

East façade of the Monastery. Sleeping cell floors are above the massive floors.

▼修道院のエントランスは北寄りにあり、3階にあたる。ピロティの上部は僧房で、下部には柔らかな曲線を描いてレセプションとミュージアムショップが展開する。

The entrance of the Monastery is well to the north on the 2nd floor. Upon the pilotis are cells for monks. Underneath ihese sleeping cells, the reception and the museum shop are stretching out.

▼シンプルの極致、「コ」形のゲートとレセプションをアプローチルートから見る。

Ultimately simple. The "U-shape" gate and the reception from the approach route.

11

平面図／Floor Plans

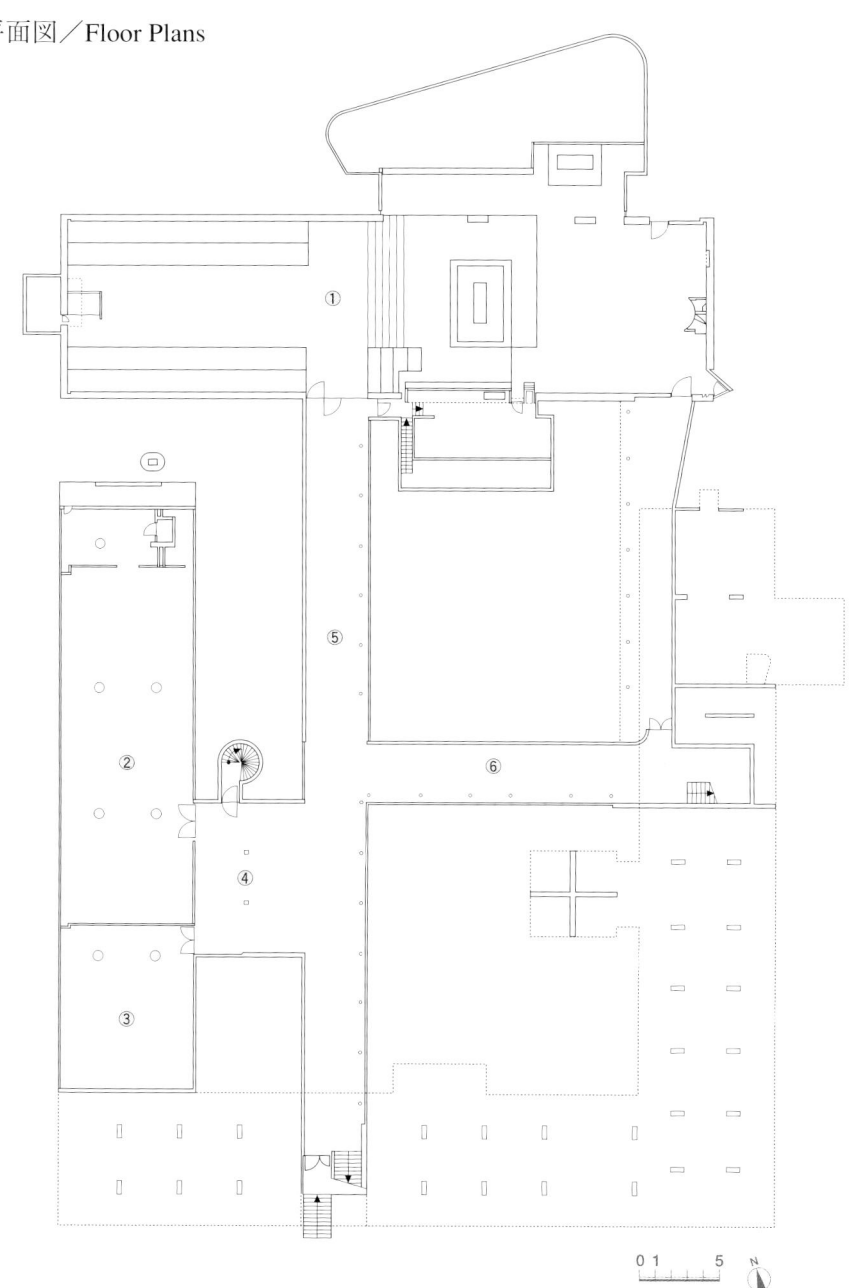

2階／First floor

①教会 ②食堂 ③参事会室 ④アトリウム ⑤大通路 ⑥小通路
①*church* ②*refectory* ③*chapter room* ④*atrium* ⑤*concourse* ⑥*alley way*

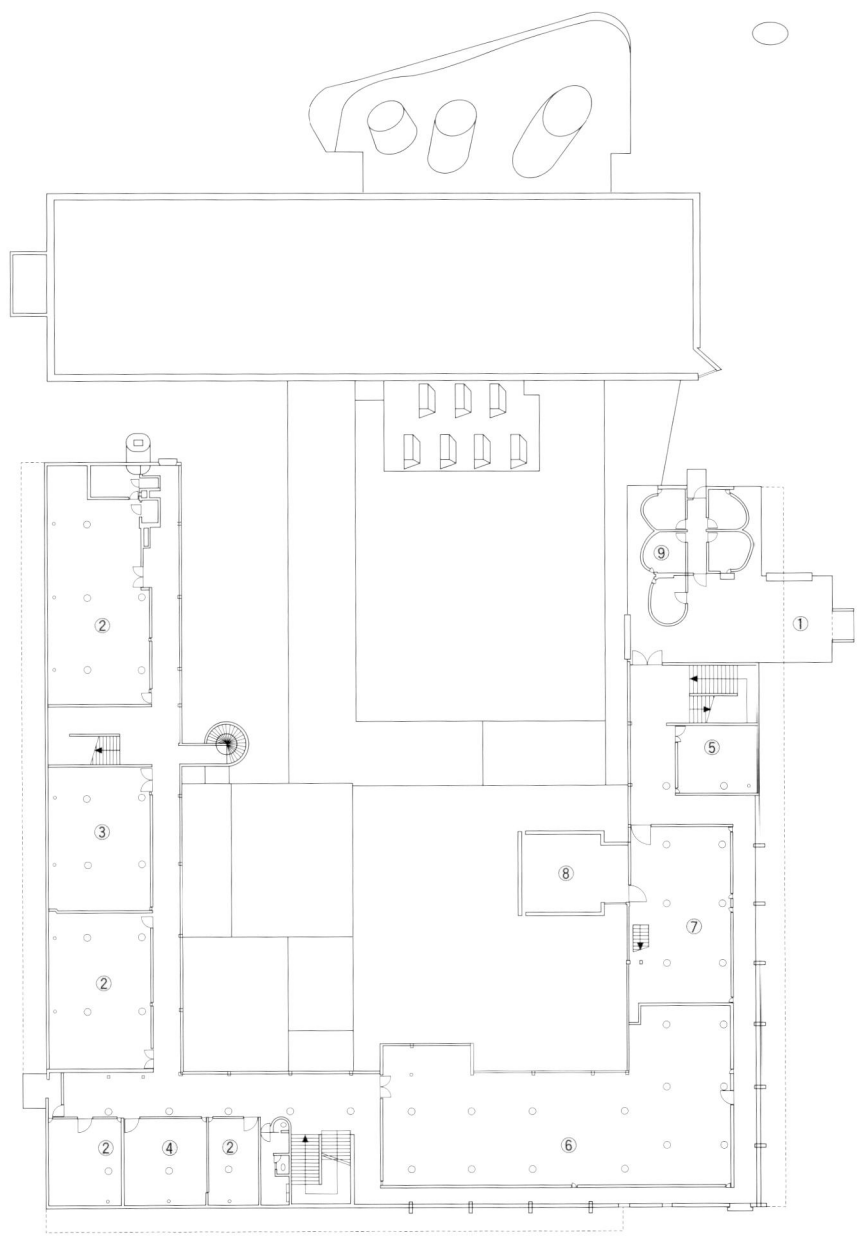

3階／Second floor

①エントランス ②教室 ③神父室 ④学生司祭室 ⑤入門修道士室 ⑥図書室 ⑦閲覧室 ⑧小礼拝堂 ⑨レセプション
①entrance ②classrooms ③priests' room ④priestling room ⑤room for convèrso ⑥library room ⑦reference room
⑧chapel ⑨reception

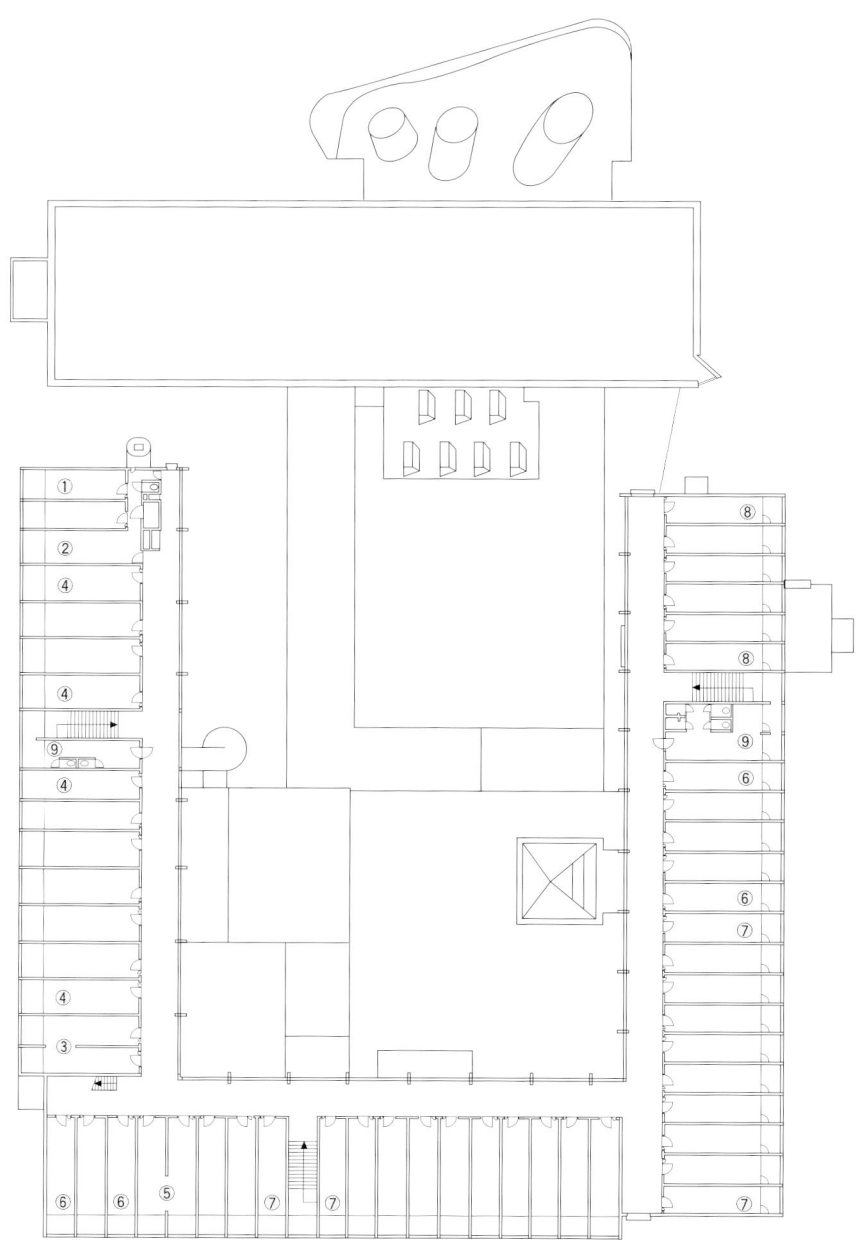

5階／Fourth floor

①病室 ②看護室 ③客室 ④教授神父用個室 ⑤補助学監神父用個室 ⑥学生司祭用個室 ⑦学生修道士用個室 ⑧入門修道士用個室 ⑨サニタリー
①*patients room* ②*nursing-care room* ③*guest room* ④*teaching father's room* ⑤*assistant principal father's room* ⑥*priestling room* ⑦*student monk's room* ⑧*room for convèrso* ⑨*sanitary room*

透視図／Axonometric Perspective

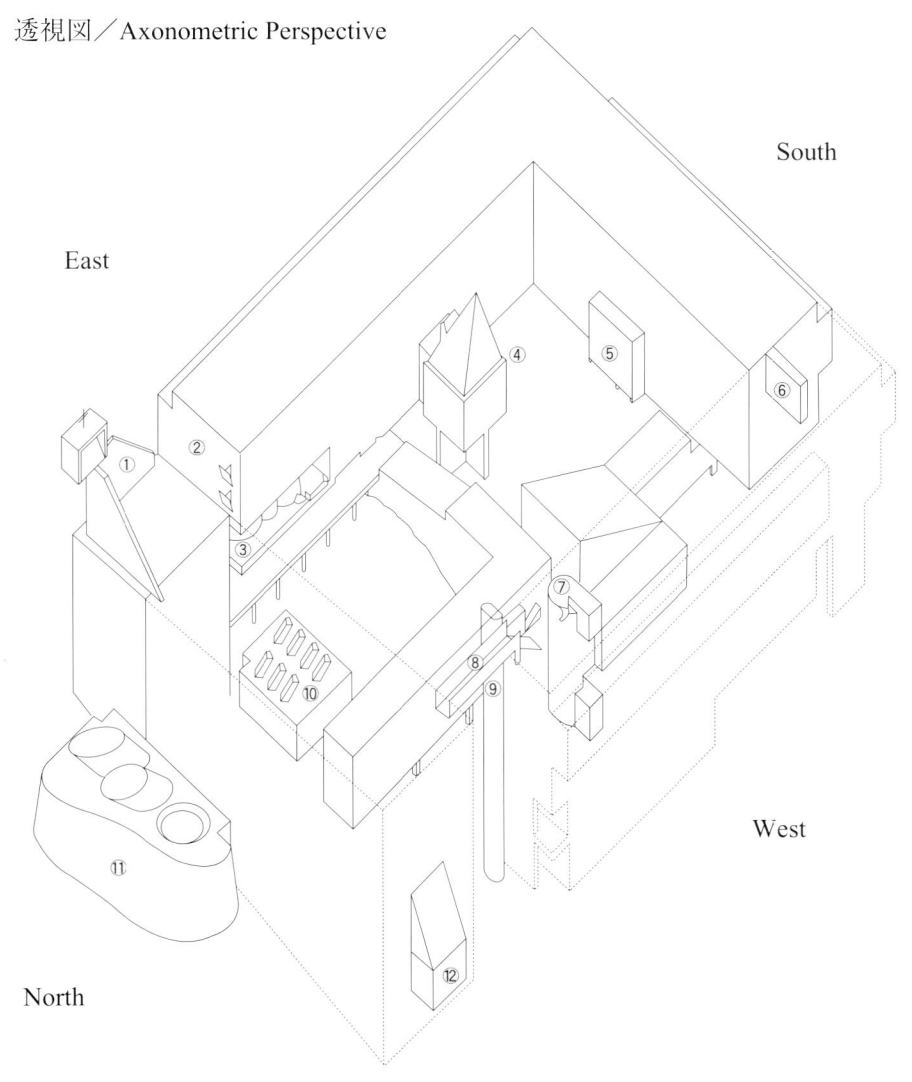

South

East

West

North

> 機能的に整理された各部分を長い回廊が結びつけている。図面と写真を引き合わせながら、豊かな想像力で散策してもらいたい。
>
> *A long cloister combines functionally-organised parts. Please take a stroll in your imagination with the plans and photographs.*

①鐘楼 ②換気の花 ③レセプション ④小礼拝堂 ⑤図書室の張り出し部分 ⑥屋根へのアクセス ⑦螺旋階段 ⑧ブリッジ ⑨煙突 ⑩聖具室 ⑪地下礼拝堂 ⑫オルガン
①*bell tower* ②*flevrs de ventilation (flower of ventilation)* ③*reception* ④*oratory* ⑤*jutting out part of the library room* ⑥*access to the roof* ⑦*spiral stairway* ⑧*bridge* ⑨*smokestack* ⑩*sacristy (storage)* ⑪*underground chapel* ⑫*organ*

▲ 僧房室内部。室内の内法幅1.8m、奥行き5.6m、天井高2.2mの個室。
標準サイズのシングルベッドで、宿泊者は自分でベッドメーキングして使う。無塗装の合板キャビネットの奥行きを利用したヘッドボードには質素なデザインのライトがついている。

Inside a sleeping cell. Internal dimension of the cell is 1.8m (width), 5.6m (depth) and 2.2m (ceiling height).
An overnight visitor makes and uses a standard-sized bed. The headboard, making use of the depth of a non-painted plywood cabinet, has a simple designed light.

▲ 共有のシャワー室の洗面器。化粧露しの温水配管が赤、給水配管が青に塗り分けられている。

Basin of a common shower room. Exposed pipes are painted red for hot-water and blue for cold water supply.

▶ デスクスタンドの明かりで両壁にウォール・ウォッシャーのような明かりのエッジができるほど狭い。正面右側がバルコニーへの扉、左側カーテン後ろに通風用の開口がある。

So narrow that the light of a desk lamp makes a bright edge like a wall washer. The right side behind is the door to the balcony and the opening behind the left-side curtains is for ventilation.

僧房階の、中庭に面する廊下。変則的な水平連続窓。方立部分（半ポンドのバターを横に立てた形）が室内側と屋外側に跳ね出す。

Hallway on the sleeping cell floor facing the garden court. Irregular long strips of ribbon windows. Mullions (shape of half-pound butter standing widthwise) are overhanging to both the inside and the outside.

4、5階の僧房階を結ぶ階段室。正面の階段上部は、右隣に位置するトイレのバルコニーから出入り可能。

Staircase connecting the sleeping cell on the 3rd and 4th floors. The top of the stairs in the front is accessible from the right-side balcony of the cloakroom.

僧房のバルコニーで切り取られた景色。拳大の黒い砕石打ち込みのPCパネルの内側はシンプルな打ち放し。手摺下部の格子は、大型PCパネルに組み込まれている。

View cut by the balcony of a sleeping cell. The inside of PC panels with fist-size black broken stone is simply exposed. The grid under the balustrade is built into large PC panels.

3階、玄関部分からトンガリ屋根の小礼拝堂にいたる通路。P7下写真の手前。

2nd floor. Alley to a chapel of the peaked roof from the entrance. Foreground of the photo in page 7.

食堂階の2階へ続く階段室。

Staircase to the refectory on the 1st floor.

▲ 縦方向に三等分された市松状のガラス面と、細いPCパネルで構成された波動ガラス面とのリズムの違いが一望できる。

Sweeping view of the contrasting rhythms of the vertically tierced checkered glasses and the undulatory-rhythm glasses consisting of thin PC panels.

2階、食堂のあるフロア。
中央奥が食堂入口。

1st floor. Behind is the refectory entrance.

宿泊見学者も利用する食堂。
最大約80名が一度に食事をすることができる。

Refectory for overnight visitors. Up to about 80 people can dine at once.

食堂前の、天井が斜めに高くつくられている部分。見付けの細いPCパネルの方立は、前衛音楽家にして構造家のクセナキス作の「音楽的配置」で構成されている。ガラス面は、あみだくじ状に分節されている。

Slanting ceiling part in front of the refectory. The thin mullions of PC panels are composed of the "musical alignment" by Xenakis, an avant-garde musician as well as a structural engineer.

▲ 聖具室に光を落とす天窓。通称「軽機関銃の天窓」。
Top light casting light on the sacristy. Popularly known as "mitraillettes" (machine gun of light).

◀ 説教壇の脇に立てられたスリムな十字架。
Thin cross standing beside the pulpit.

▲ 聖堂内部を西側（パイプオルガンのある側）から見る。正面に説教壇、右に入口、その奥に聖具室と「軽機関銃の天窓」。右奥の縦スリットは、外観ではそれほどインパクトのあるものではないが、内部では劇的な闇と光の演出世界を支えている。目が慣れるまではかなり暗い。

The holy shrine inside from the west (where there is a chamber organ). The front is the pulpit, the entrance on the right and the sacristy and the "machine gun of light" behind. The right-side behind the vertical slit is not so inspirational outside, but it's an inevitable factor for the staging of the darkness and the light inside. You cannot see well until your eyes get used to the darkness.

▷ 聖堂のサイドチャペル。通称「大砲の天窓」。ここは、聖堂の北側の巨大な壁面の下部に、グランドピアノのように張り出した低層部。3本のシリンダーが貫入し、その部分が巨大な天窓となる。その下部、一番明るい部分にマッシブな祭壇が配置する。内部を原色に塗装された天窓からの光は、思いのほかしっくりと調和している。

The side chapel of the holy shrine. Commonly called "canons a lumiere" (cannons of light). This is, looking from the outside, a lower part, which projecting like a grand piano under the large wall of the north-side of the holy shrine. Three cylinders are piercing the ceiling and they become large top lights. Underneath them, the massive altar is located in the brightest area. Surprisingly, the light from the top lights painted in primary colours harmonize here.

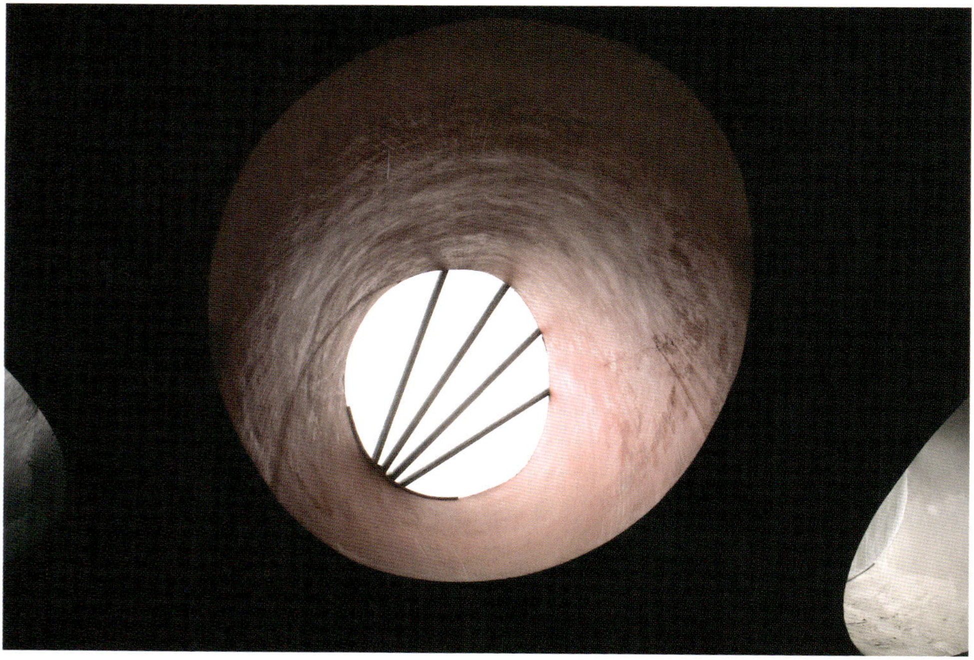

▲ 3つある「大砲の天窓」の中央を見上げる。

Looking up the middle of the "cannons of light".

▲ 「大砲の天窓」から降る光は、聖堂階とその下の地下聖堂階を照らす。地下聖堂へは聖具室脇から、礼拝堂を横切る地下通路経由。

Light falling down from the "cannons of light" illuminates the holy shrine floor and the underground holy shrine floor. You can access the underground holy shrine by way of an underground passage across the monastery from the side of the sacrarium.

▲ 説教壇からパイプオルガンのある西側壁面を見る。照明計画とは「闇をデザインすること」であるが、聖堂の自然採光も、照明計画に似て、「闇の配置」に気が配られている。光の通る開口部の面積比率を限定し、効果を上げる。パイプオルガン置場は、西側外壁を貫いて張り出している。宿泊見学者には朝のミサに参加することを強くお勧めしたい。

Looking at the west-side wall with the chamber organ from the pulpit. Lighting program is "designing the darkness" and the natural lighting of the holy shrine is programmed with much attention to "layout of the darkness". The areas of openings where light goes through are limited so that the effects of them are enhanced. The place for the chamber organ is projecting through the west-side wall. I would strongly recommend overnight visitors should attend a morning mass.

▲ 3〜5階の中庭に面する通路の「水平連続窓」。方立が水平に膨張して内外に飛び出す形状。外部は横に細長い窓の中にあって外壁に影を落とし、アクセントとなる。

"Long strips of ribbon windows" of the alley from the 2nd to the 4th floors facing the garden court. Mullions are expanding horizontally to project to both sides. They make shadows outside to draw attention while the ribbon windows are narrow and long.

▲ 3階西側の教室の外部、中庭に面する回廊。

Outside of the west-side classrooms on the 2nd floor. The cloister faces the garden court.

◀ 食堂から聖堂にいたる聖堂のメインの入口。100mmを超える厚さのスチール製の縦軸回転の大型扉。さらにその一部に「子扉」が組み込まれ少人数の出入りに対応する。

Main entrance of the holy shrine from the refectory. Great revolving steel door of more than 100mm thickness. A "small door" is built in to deal with the incomings and outgoings of smaller groups.

31

▸ 3階入口の南部、小礼拝堂の前室の壁に紙で切り抜かれた原寸の「モデュロール」。

The south part of the entrance on the 2nd floor. Full-sized "Modulor" of paper on the wall of the anterior chamber of the chapel.

▸ 小礼拝堂内部。中庭に面するトンガリ屋根は、この修道院のデザイン・モチーフとなった「ル・トロネ修道院」を彷彿（ほうふつ）とさせる。ウォール・ウォッシャーとなる天窓からのスリット採光。

Inside the chapel. Peaked roof facing the garden court bring back the picture of the "Abbaye du Thoronet", a design motif of this Monastery. Slit lighting from the top light becoming a wall washer.

▸ 内部壁面の多くの部分は、大粒のコンクリート吹き付けの上、白色ペイント仕上げ。

Many parts of interior walls are finished with white paint that is painted onto concrete that has been sprayed onto the walls.

▲ 東側僧房階の下部、3階の閲覧室外側の「水平連続窓」外部。
Bottom of the east sleeping cell floor. Outside the "long strips of ribbon windows" of the reference room on the 2nd floor.

▲ 螺旋階段の階段室の屋根と装飾性の高い雨樋。
Roof of the staircase of the spiral stairway and the rain gutter with profuse decoration.

▲ 日没前、僧房階から北方向を望む。スカイライン
を鋭角に切り裂くのは、小礼拝堂の屋根。
この修道院が完成した時から変わらない光景。

Before the sunset. The north direction from the sleeping cell floor. The roof of the chapel outlined against the skyline.
The changeless view since the completion of the Monastery.

▲ スイス学生会館やユニテ・ダビタシオンの膨らみのあるピロティ柱とは違い、厚板を切り抜いたような、自由曲線のくし型の柱が唐突に登場する。

Free curve comb-shape columns, not like the swelling piloti columns of the Pavillion Suisse or the Unité d'Habitation, appear suddenly.

▲ 北側外観。聖堂の北側に飛び出した「大砲の天窓」を戴く地下礼拝堂部分。
North appearance. Underground chapel, projecting to the north of the holy shrine, with the "cannons of light" on top.

▲ 南側外観。左奥にラルブレールの集落が拡がる。
South appearance. Spreading left behind are the settlements of L'Arbresle.

Detail

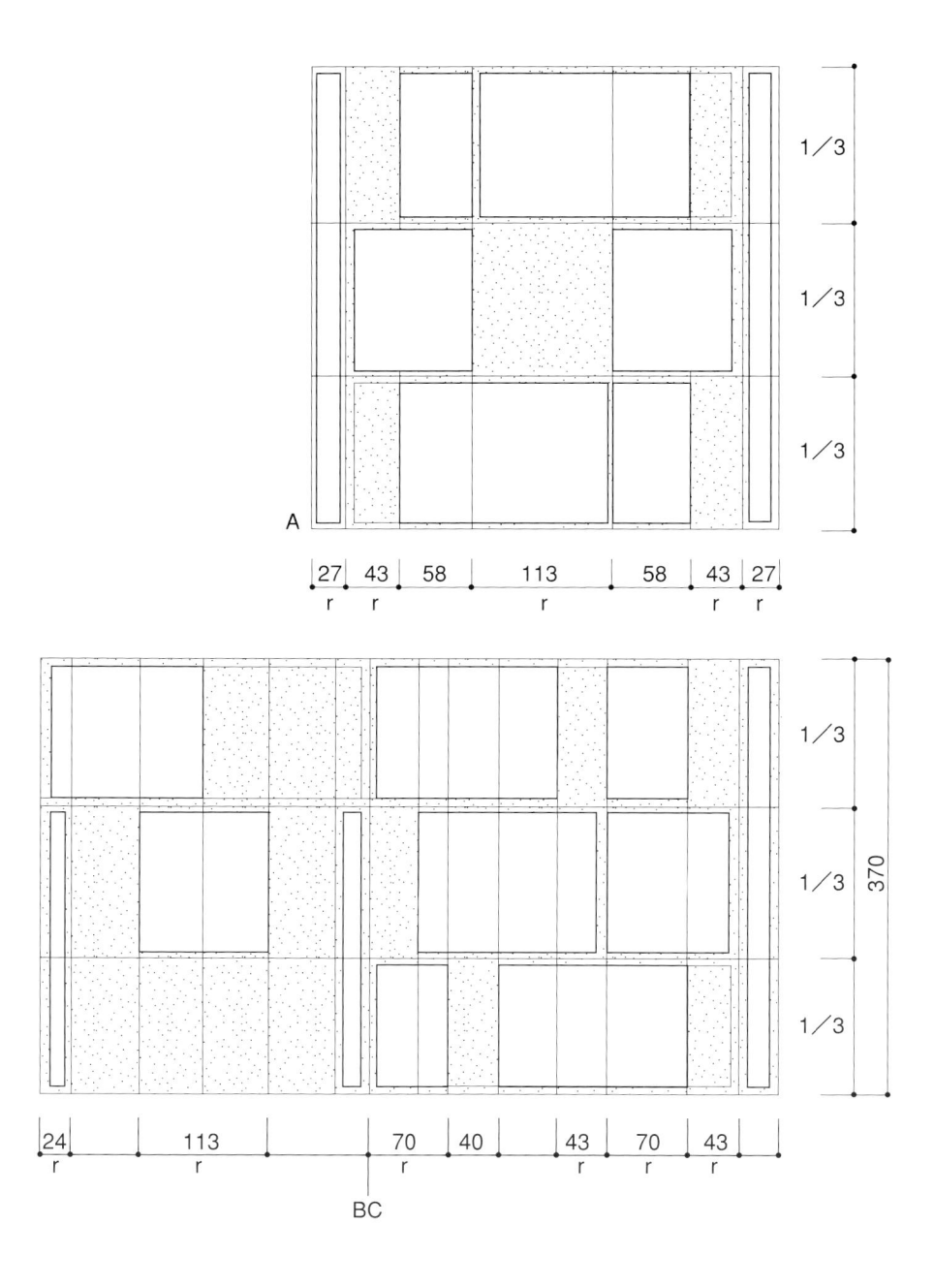

A

| 27 | 43 | 58 | 113 | 58 | 43 | 27 |
| r | r | | r | | r | r |

1/3
1/3
1/3

| 24 | 113 | 70 | 40 | 43 | 70 | 43 |
| r | r | r | | r | r | r |

BC

1/3
1/3
1/3

370

38

入口階、玄関から中庭を望む。手前の通路が波動リズムガラス面（オンデュラトワール）、奥が市松状のPCパネル（H1パネル）。

Entrance floor. Looking at the garden court from the entrance. Foreground alley has the undulatory-rhythm glass walls (ondulatoire) and behind has the PC panels (H1 Panel).

市松状のPCパネル。
A→上：H1パネル。19のタイプあり。
B→下左：Z1パネル。3タイプあり。
C→下右：Z2パネル。7タイプあり。
このように多くのタイプがあり、かなり「現場泣かせ」であったことが想像される。

Checkered PC panels.
A → Top：H1 Panel. 19 types.
B → Bottom left：Z1 Panel. 3 types.
C → Bottom right：Z2 Panel. 7 types.
There are a number of types like these. These would have been the bane of the construction site.

市松状PCパネルの内側からの景色。
View from the inside of the checkered PC panels.

39

修道院の原点を強く意識した
巨匠の円熟期の大冒険

修道院の立地

　中南部フランスの中心都市、人口約45万のリヨン。シャルル・ド・ゴール空港からTGVで約2時間、世界的なグルメの街である。さらにリヨンから西に延びるSNCF（国鉄）で西へ約40分。ラルブレール（L'Arbresle）駅がル・コルビュジェ晩年の代表作ラ・トゥーレット修道院の最寄り駅である。

　切符を売る駅員はいても改札には立たない。無人駅寸前のような静かな駅前には、当然のようにタクシー乗場などは存在しない。修道院へ自動車などで行くことなど想像できなかった時代と同じ方法で詣でる事が、重要な意味を持つ。

　そもそも修道院とは、カトリックの若い僧の修行の場、その起源において、本来は禁欲、勤勉、質素を旨とし、ひたすら宗教上の徳を積む場である。そのような場所が、中心市街地の近くにあることは考えにくい。事実、修道院の立地は、俗界とは隔絶した場所であることが多い。極端な例としてギリシアのメテオラ[※1]（世界遺産）のように、尖った岩山の頂上に作られたものもある。

　メテオラほどではないにしても、簡単に行けてしまうと、ありがたみが少ない。身体にはきつくても、徒歩によるアプローチが宗教施設を訪ねる心の準備には好ましい。悪天候下であれば、傑出した修道院との出会いはさらに劇的となる。

建築的主張の発展形

　コルビュジェが唱えた「近代建築五原則」は、ここラ・トゥーレット修道院でも見事に全項目が実践されている。ただし、壮年期の代表作であるサヴォア邸（1931年竣工）で実践されたものと、円熟期の代表作であるラ・トゥーレット修道院（1960年竣工）では30年の隔たりがあり、当然のことながら五原則の出現の様相が異なっている。

　改めて五原則を示すと、①ピロティ、②屋上庭園、③自由な平面、④独立骨組みにより可能になった水平連続窓、⑤自由な立面である。

　①ピロティは、初期のラ・ロッシュ邸（1923）やサヴォア邸では控えめであったものが、スイス学生会館（1930）、マルセイユ

※1 メテオラ
ギリシア北西部、セサリア地方北端の奇岩群とその上に建設された修道院共同体、14世紀に成立。その景観とギリシア正教修道院文化の価値から世界遺産に登録。撮影：西村博之©

Meteora
*A group of monasteries built on top of strange rocks and the area in the 14th century at the north end of the Thessaly in the northern west Greece. They have been on the list of the World Heritages of UNESCO due to its scenery and cultural uniqueness as Greek Orthodoxy monasteries.
(Photo:©Hiroyuki Nishimura)*

40

Strong Awareness of the Origin of a Monastery Odyssey of the Master Architect in His Mature Age

Location of the Monastery

Lyon, the central city in South-Central France, is about 2 hours distance from the Charles de Gaulle International Airport by TGV. It is a world-known gourmet city with about 450,000 in population. Another 40 minutes SNCF (French railway) train ride will take you to "L'arbresle", the nearest station to the Monastery of La Tourette, which represents Le Corbusier's later years.

There is a station attendant selling tickets though nobody is standing at the gate. There are, of course, no taxi stands in front of an almost ghost station like this one. It is very meaningful to visit a monastery in a similar way as people did in the old days when they never imagined going there by car.

A monastery is, from its origin, a place where younger Catholic monks mainly cultivate religious virtue. Main concepts are abstinence, diligence and frugality. Therefore, such a place isn't likely to be located around the city centre. Actually, many monasteries are isolated from the secular world. Meteora[*1], a group of monasteries (one of the World Heritage sites of UNESCO), built upon the craggy mountain, can be an extreme example.

We will appreciate a monastery more, if the location isn't easily accessible, even if not as hard as Meteora. A walking approach will be better to access such religious institutions. In addition, adverse weather conditions will make the encounter even more dramatic.

Development of Architectural Assertion

All of the "Five Points towards a New Architecture" of Le Corbusier are realised in fine style at this Monastery of La Tourette. At the same time, you can identify different complexities of these practices due to the flight of time; 30 years between the "Villa Savoye" (completed in 1931) in his late middle age and the "Monastery of La Tourette" (completed in 1960) in his mature age.

Again, the Five Points are; (1) pilotis, (2) roof garden, (3) an open floor plan, (4) long strips of ribbon windows without concern for supporting walls and (5) free façade.

(1): Pilotis were relatively restrained in his early works such as the Maison La Roche (1923) or the Villa Savoye. However, these pilotis became massive at the Pavillion Suisse (1930) and the Unité

上：サヴォア邸
中：スイス学生会館
下：ユニテ・ダビタシオン
　　（マルセイユ）
　　下のみリネア建築企画©

Top: Villa Savoye
Middle: Pavillion Suisse
Bottom: Unité d'Habitation
(Marseille) Linea CO.,LTD©

のユニテ・ダビタシオン（1945）を経て大規模なものとなり、ラ・トゥーレット修道院の南面では斜面敷地にあり、教室・学生司祭室を最大で9m近く持ち上げている。

④については、サヴォア邸の時代は、初期のプロトタイプともいうべき純粋でシンプルな構成となっているが、ラ・トゥーレット修道院では、先に述べた波動リズムガラス面が、ひとひねりふたひねり加えた発展形を見せている。⑤に関しては、2、3階の中庭側の立面に多用されている細い線でガラス枠が構成されたPCコンクリートパネルによる市松状のユニットが、コンセプトと技術力の成長発展形の力強さをアピールしている。

ラ・トゥーレット修道院の座標

ル・コルビュジェの代表作を3つ挙げるとすると、ほぼ誰しも異論のないところが、サヴォア邸（1928）とロンシャンの礼拝堂（1950）、そしてラ・トゥーレット修道院（1953）。もしも、「代表作にあと3つ」ということであれば、大学都市のスイス学生会館（1930）、マルセイユのユニテ・ダビタシオン（1945）、そしてチャンディガールの一群の建築（1953～59）というところか。

それらの中でもモダニズムの傑出したドグマである「近代建築五原則」の典型的な応用例という切り口で選ぶなら、初期の作品であるサヴォア邸、円熟期のユニテ・ダビタシオン（マルセイユ）、そして晩年のラ・トゥーレット修道院というところである。

ラ・トゥーレット修道院以前のコルビュジェ作品をご存知で、まだ実物をご覧になっていない人に、この建物の説明を要求される状況があるとしよう。

「ラ・トゥーレット修道院とは、"長方形のロンシャン礼拝堂"に、"コの字型のユニテ・ダビタシオン"を連結して全体が『ロの字型プラン』で構成されたものだ」。

図面や写真を使わず、この説明で本質に迫ることができる。

モダニズムの旗手として、「近代建築五原則」を唱えた改革者としてのコルビュジェの人物像から、サヴォア邸→ユニテ・ダビタシオン→チャンディガールという一連の作風は自然に理解できる。

しかしながら同時進行で生み出されたロンシャンの礼拝堂が、それらとはあまりに別次元、別路線の彫刻風であったために、それ自体の造形的完成度の高さと相俟ってより多くの感動を呼んだ。

マッシブなコンクリートの圧倒的ボリュームと、開口部から飛び

ル・コルビュジェ作品の系譜と「近代建築五原則」主要作品

1914 ドミノ型住宅の研究
1922 画家オザンファンの住宅
1923 ラ・ロッシュ/ジャンヌレ邸
1924 エスプリ・ヌーヴォー館
1926 救世軍人民院
1927 ヴァイセンホフ・ジードルンクシュトゥットガルト
1928 サヴォア邸*
1929 救世軍難民院
1930 大学都市のスイス学生会館
1936 保険教育館
1936 パリ国際博・新時代館
1945 ユニテ・ダビタシオン*
　　　（マルセイユ）
1949 クルチェット邸
1950 ロンシャンの礼拝堂*
1951 ショーダン邸
1952 ユニテ・ダビタシオン
　　　（レゼ・レ・ナント）
1953 総合庁舎*
1953 ラ・トゥーレット修道院*
1953 大学都市のブラジル学生会館
1955 州会議事堂*
1956 スタディアム
1956 ユニテ・ダビタシオン
　　　（ブリエ・アン・フォレ）
1956 青年文化の家
1957 ユニテ・ダビタシオン
　　　（ベルリン）
1957 西洋美術館
1959 美術学校
1960 ユニテ・ダビタシオン
　　　（フィルミニ）
<表中の*は筆者推薦の6件、ロンシャン以外は「近代建築五原則（またはその一部）」の顕著な応用例>
年数は、設計完了年。コルビュジェ財団資料より

Chronology of Le Corbusier Works and the "Five Points towards a New Architecture" Major Works

1914 theoretical studies on the "Domino" House
1922 Atelier Ozenfant
1923 Maison La Roche- Jeanneret
1924 Pavillion de L'Esprit Nouveau
1926 Annexe du Palais du Peuple
1927 Villas at Weissenhof Estate, Stuttgart
1928 Villa Savoye **
1929 Cité de Refuge
1930 Pavillion Suisse, Cité Universitaire
1936 Palace of Ministry of National Education and Public Health
1936 Pavillion, Paris Exposition
1945 Unité d'Habitation (Marseille) **
1949 Curutchet House
1950 Chapelle Notre Dame du Haut, Ronchamp **
1951 Villa Shodhan
1952 Unité d'Habitation (Nantes-Rezé, Nantes)
1953 Secretariat **
1953 Monastery of La Tourette **
1953 Pavillion du Bréil, Cité Universitaire
1955 Assembly Building (Parliament) **
1956 Stade
1956 Unité d'Habitation (Briey en Forê)
1956 La Maison des Jeunes et de la Culture
1957 Unité d'Habitation (Berlin)
1957 National Museum of Western Art
1959 College of Art
1960 Unité d'Habitation (Firminy)

*<6 works with * are recommended by the author. Explicit application of the "Five Points towards a New Architecture"*
(or some points of these) except for the Ronchamp>
Adscript year shows the completion of each building. Source material from the Foundation Le Corbusier.

d'Habitation (Marseille) (1945), and, lastly, lifting up the classrooms and priestling rooms of the Monastery of La Tourette for almost 9m on the southern slope area.

Regarding (4), long strips of ribbon windows at the Villa Savoye era were simple and prototype-like although those of the Monastery show some developments with abovementioned undulatory-rhythm glass walls. As for (5), free façade, checkered units of PC concrete with glasses of thin frames, frequently used for the garden court side of the 1st and 2nd floors, show the vigorous developments of his theories and techniques.

Positioning the Monastery of La Tourette

Almost all the answers would be the Villa Savoye (1928), the Chapelle Notre Dame du Haut, Ronchamp (1950) and the Monastery of La Tourette (1953) if you asked somebody to choose the three best works of Le Corbusier. "Another 3 best ones" might be the Pavillion Suisse, Cité Universitaire (1930), the Unité d'Habitation (Marseille) (1945) and the series of architectures in Chandigarh (1953-59).

Among these, the Villa Savoye at an early phase, the Unité d'Habitation (Marseille) in his mature career and the Monastery of La Tourette in later life could be highlighted as advanced examples of "five points towards a new architecture", the modernism dogma of the first magnitude.

And now, how would you describe the Monastery of La Tourette to somebody who had seen the works of Le Corbusier other than this Monastery building?

"The Monastery of La Tourette is an 'O-shape combination', made up of the 'rectangular Chapelle Notre Dame du Haut, Ronchamp' and 'U-shape Unité d'Habitation'".

This explanation shows the essences of the Monastery even without a plan or a photograph.

You can easily understand the set of trends from the Villa Savoye to the Chandigarh buildings through the Unité d'Habitation if you see the reformist portrait of Le Corbusier as a standard-bearer of the modernism.

The Chapelle Notre Dame du Haut, Ronchamp, produced at the same time as these, caused a most agreeable sensation because it was in just another dimension and had an inspirational and completed shape like a sculpture.

The same architect of these two trends configured both tastes in one architectural shape as the Monastery of La Tourette; a dominant volume of massive concrete and colourful lighting of the Chapelle Notre Dame du Haut, Ronchamp and a highly elevated complex

43

込んでくる色光というロンシャンの礼拝堂の路線と、開放的なピロティで複合的住戸ユニットを高々と持ち上げているユニテ・ダビタシオンの路線の両者が、双方の作者である建築家により、ラ・トゥーレット修道院で、ひとつの建築形態に構成された。

技法のブラッシュアップ

晩年の作品であるラ・トゥーレット修道院は、コルビュジェが実作で様々な経験を積む中で、自家薬籠中のものとしてきたものの集大成であることに、間違いはない。さらに、巨匠の巨匠たる所以のひとつであるが、それまでに採用済みの技法のブラッシュアップに加えて、別分野で際立った才能をもつ若いスタッフを抜擢して、それまでのどの建築においても存在しなかった大型開口部のデザイン処理、すなわち「波動ガラス面」もしくは「音楽的ガラス面」をつくりだしていることが特筆に価する。

聖堂への自然光の取り入れ方や修道院部分の窓割りなど、ここだけのオリジナルの手法が採用されていることに関し、突出したひらめきに圧倒される。

デザインソースは日本建築?

1924年、ユトレヒトに誕生したリートフェルト作品のシュレーダーハウス[※2]は、日本建築の「田の字型間取り」の明確な応用例であった。ル・コルビュジェの「近代建築五原則」の根幹をなす独立骨組み「ドミノシステム[※3]」にしても、壁がなくとも建築が存在できるという西洋人にとっては大いなるパラダイム・シフトである。そのデザインソースが、柱と屋根だけで建築が存在しうる極東の伝統建築、具体的には東屋[※4]の系列であるとすると、こちらも秀逸な日本の伝統的技法の応用展開事例である。

ジヴェルニーのモネ屋敷の膨大な浮世絵コレクションをはじめ、セザンヌ、ゴーギャン、ロートレックなど印象派の多くの巨匠たちが、こぞって浮世絵版画に傾倒した。多くの分野でのボーダレス傾向は歴史が古い。

「ドミノシステム」のデザインソースが日本建築であるとコルビュジェ本人が告白してはいないが、そうでないことを証明することのほうがよほど困難であろう。

西洋の建築家の日本研究、それを換骨奪胎した成果が、世界の建築の歴史を変えた。ナチス・ドイツに目をつけられて仕事がしにくくなり、ドイツを脱出。1933年に支持者のいた日本に流れ着

※2 シュレーダーハウス
トーマス・リートフェルト設計のシュレーダーハウスは、1924年に竣工。赤、青、黄を基調とした、デ・ステイル建築の最も知られたもの。オランダ、ユトレヒトにあり2000年に世界遺産に登録される。

Schroder House
The Schroder House designed by G. T. Rietveld was completed in 1924. One of the most popular architecture of "De Stijl" (the style), in which the main colour palette was reduced to the primary colours red, yellow and blue. This building in Utrecht, the Netherlands has been on the list of the World Heritages from 2000.

※4 東屋
庭園などに休憩所や展望所として建てられた柱だけの壁のない小屋。

Japanese arbour
A cottage with only columns (without walls) for a rest or a view in the garden.

housing units upon the pilotis of the Unité d'Habitation.

Brushup of Techniques

It is obvious that his later work La Tourette Monastery was a summarisation of what Le Corbusier had acquired through a number of practices. In addition, it is worth noting he not only adopted already-applied skills, but attempted and created a new technique of "undulatory-rhythm glass walls" or "musical glass walls" with a young talented staff from another field. This is why he is the master of masters.

Sparks of genius, which can be seen only here, simply overwhelm us, such as how to bring natural light into the cathedral and the arrangement of the windows at the monastery part.

Japanese Architecture as Design Sources?

The Schroder House[*2] (G. T. Rietveld, 1924) in Utrecht was an obvious application of "O-shape room layout" of Japanese architecture. The "Domino" house[*3], a foundation for Le Corbusier's "five points towards a new architecture", enabling an existence of architecture without walls, was a great paradigm shift for Westerners. This system also might be a brilliant development of Japanese traditional techniques in that the design sources for this system may have been a traditional architecture in the Far East, such as a Japanese arbour[*4].

All the great painters of the Impressionism made a commitment to Ukiyoe, or Japanese wood block prints, such as Monet, who had a great collection of Ukiyoe at a villa in Giverny, Cezanne, Gauguin and Lautrec. Various branches have a long history of a borderless tendency.

It'd be challenging if you tried to deny that the design sources for the "Domino" house should be Japanese architecture, although Le Corbusier himself did not admit that.

A Western architect's studies on Japan and the results as he absorbed changed the architectural history of the world. Escaping from Germany since it became difficult for him to work due to the attention by the Nazis, in 1933, Bruno Taut[*5] reached Japan, where he had supporters. He severely criticised the Nikko Toshogu Temple, though he highly praised the Katsura Imperial Villa, at the same time. These illustrations bear fruit as the "Nihonbi-no-Saihakken." (Rediscovery of Japanese Beauty published by Iwanami Shoten) Confirming the essences of "Japanese beauty" demonstrated by a

---

※3 ドミノシステム
伝統的な西洋の建築の工法は、石を積んで壁を作り、その上に床や屋根を構成する「組積造」で、建築にとって壁は必須だったが、コルビュジェは鉄筋コンクリートの「床と柱と階段のみの工法」を考案。壁がなくても建築が成立することを実証した。

The Domino House
Le Corusier invented an open floor plan consisting of "only slabs, columns and a stairway" of reinforced concrete though walls were thought to be necessary in traditional Western architecture. The mainstream was the "stone masonry", heaping up stones to build up walls to consist of floors or roofs on top of them. But, Le Corbusier demonstrated that architecture can be realised without walls.

※5 ブルーノ・タウト
建築家、都市計画家。ドイツ生まれ。(1880-1938) ジャポニズム、アールヌーボーを通して日本に関心をもつ。桂離宮と日光東照宮を対比させ、前者に日本の伝統美を見出し、『ニッポン』『日本美の再発見』などを著した。数寄屋造りの中にモダニズム建築に通じる近代性があることを評価し、日本人建築家に伝統と近代という問題について大きな影響を与えた。

Bruno Taut
Architect and urban planner, born in Germany (1880-1938). Taut became interested in Japan through Japonism and Art Nouveau and contrasted the Katsura Imperial Villa and the Nikko Toshogu Temple to find traditional Japanese beauty in the former. He produced some influential books on Japanese culture such as "Nippon" and "Nihonbi-no-Saihakken" (Rediscovery of Japanese beauty). Taut surmised that Sukiya style, the style of a tea-ceremony house, has modernity connecting to modernism architecture, having a large impact on Japanese architects about the tradition and the modern.

いたブルーノ・タウト※5。日光東照宮を酷評し、その一方で桂離宮を絶賛し、そのあたりが著書『日本美の再発見』(岩波新書)に結実した。謙虚な日本人は、外圧で指摘された「日本美」の真髄を追認するかたちで、ドイツの大建築家の託宣を喜び賞賛した。しかしながら、桂離宮を見て、ミース※6やグロピウス※7が唱え実践してきたモダニズムの精神、その典型である標語「Less is more」を、彼らよりも300年も早く実現していた日本人の技量に、タウトは恐れ慄いたのではないか？ 桂離宮の雁行する高床の書院がピロティの原型に見えなくもない。桂離宮には、屋上庭園以外の「五原則」が揃っている。

傑出したプロデューサー

クテュリエ神父は、後にコルビュジェの2大代表作となるロンシャンの礼拝堂およびラ・トゥーレット修道院のプロデュースをした人物として名を残す。

実はこの人物はただの宗教者ではない。彼は青年時代に芸術家としての教育を受け、RC構造の世界初の建築への大規模な応用例として名高いパリ16区の「フランクリン街のアパート」や、パリ東部郊外の「ル・ランシー教会※8」の設計者として世界中に知られるオーギュスト・ペレの事務所(コルビュジェも在籍したことがある)に籍を置いていた。打ち放しコンクリートの教会建築への最初の応用例として知られるル・ランシー教会のステンドグラスの制作にもたずさわった。つまりコルビュジェとは修行時代の事務所の同窓生という縁がある。クテュリエ神父は当時の有名画家、アンリ・マティス、フェルナン・レジェ、パブロ・ピカソ、売れっ子の建築家ロベール・マレ・ステヴァンとも親交があった。

芸術に関する目利きの神父は、コルビュジェの傑出した才能を正しく評価できる立場にあった。実はコルビュジェはほとんど無神論者であったといわれている。神父はその著書の中で「キリスト教芸術のルネサンスのためには、天才的芸術家であり、かつ聖者であるような人物が存在するのが理想的である」「この復興のため、才能のない信者よりも才能のある天才に助けを求めるほうがより確かだと思われる」と記している。建築家にとって、なんともありがたい話ではないか。

コルビュジェはその頃、既に世界的に名が知れ、設計の依頼が引きもきらない中、同窓生であり、クライアント代表者としてのアドバンテージが、プロジェクトの進行中に建設工事費の膨張な

日本三名園の岡山後楽園にある流店。竣工は1700年。神社の拝殿や舞殿のように柱のみで成り立つ平屋ではなく、一階が柱だけで上部に階がある構造。ピロティやドミノシステムの原型に見える。撮影：よしだまき◎

Ryuten, in the Okayama Korakuen, one of the three major gardens of Japan. Completed in 1700. The Ryuten structure has only columns on the ground floor with an upper floor on top of it, not like a one-storied building of only columns such as Haiden, an altar, or Maiden, a hall for sacred dance and music in a shrine. This looks like a prototype of pilotis or the Domino house.
(Photo:©Maki Yoshida)

※8 ル・ランシー教会
オーギュスト・ペレ設計による20世紀最初の鉄筋コンクリート打ち放しのノートルダム教会、1923年竣工。32本の独立した細い円柱があり、外壁一面にステンドグラスが設置されている。

Notre Dame du Raincy
Designed by Auguste Perret and completed in 1923, this Notre Dame is the first application of exposed reinforced concrete for a church in the 20th century. The Notre Dame has 32 independent thin cylinders and stained glasses all over the outside walls.

[*6] ミース・ファン・デル・ローエ
建築家。ドイツ生まれ。(1886-1969)。"Less is more"（無駄な部分を削ぎ落としたデザインが、より豊かなデザインである）という標語で知られ、インターナショナル・スタイルの成立に貢献した近代建築の巨匠。自由な間取りのユニヴァーサル・スペースという概念を提示し、トゥーゲンハット邸、ファンズワース邸は今でも住宅の珠玉。

Ludwig Mies van der Rohe
Architect. Born in Germany. (1886-1969). Coined the phrase "Less is more". One of the most influential masterminds of the International Style, he praised the concept of the open "universal space", concretized by works such as the Tugendhat House, and the Farnsworth House.

[*7] ヴァルター・グロピウス
建築家。ドイツ生まれ。(1883-1969) バウハウスの創立者で、1919年から1928年まで初代校長を務めた。グロピウスが著書『国際建築』で主張した発想がもとになり、1930年代にアメリカで提唱されたインターナショナル・スタイル（国際様式）が生まれた。

Walter Adolph Georg Gropius
Architect. Born in Germany. (1883-1969). Gropius was a founder of Bauhaus and was appointed as master of the school from 1919 to 1928. His concepts of "International Architecture" lead to the International Style in the 1930s in the U.S.A.

foreigner's perspective, humble Japanese were pleased to welcome the novel ideas from the great German architect. Nevertheless, might Taut himself fear the techniques of Japanese, who practiced, even 300 years earlier than Mies[*6] or Gropius[*7], the spirits of the modernism and its typical mantra "less is more"? You could regard the upper class high-floored writing room of the Katsura Imperial Villa as the prototype of pilotis. The Katsura Imperial Villa has all the "five points" except a roof garden.

Outstanding Producer

The Father Couturier is renowned as the producer of the Chapelle Notre Dame du Haut, Ronchamp and the Monastery of La Tourette, which became two major works of Le Corbusier.

Not only was he a priest was he. Couturier was educated as an artist in his adolescent years and belonged to the office of world-known architect Auguste Perret, where Le Corbusier used to work as well. Works of Auguste Perret include the Apartment, rue Franklin (Paris, 16e) and the Notre Dame du Raincy in the eastern suburb of Paris[*8].

Couturier worked on the stained glass of the Notre Dame du Raincy. This building is famous as the first application of exposed concrete for a church. The Father and Le Corbusier have a connection in that they were working at the same office in their youthful days. The Father Couturier's friendship also includes Henri Matisse, Fernand Léger, Pablo Picasso and Robert Mallet Stevens.

The Father was able to appraise the preeminent talent of Le Corbusier, since the former was a good judge of art, too. Actually, Le Corbusier was said to be an almost atheist. The Father wrote in his publication that it is ideal that there exists a person like a saint and talented artist at the same time for the renaissance of Christian art. He put forward it looked like help from a talented genius would be more reliable than one from an untalented believer. What a boon to an architect!

Le Corbusier was already famous on a global basis and there were more and more clients in an endless stream. Under such circumstances, the advantage of the client representative, being old office friends at the same time, paid off for both the planner and the client although there were ups and downs such as an expansion of construction costs.

どの紆余曲折はあったものの、設計者にとっても発注者側代表にとっても幸せな結果をもたらした。

音楽家で構造家でもあるクセナキス

　緩やかな丘陵の70haの敷地に建つ修道院は、登りの山道を北北東方向からアクセスする。主要な前面道路は東側だが、この修道院は4周ぐるりと「引き」がとれる位置にあり、道が周囲を取りまく状況でつくられているため、4面がそれぞれ「正面」と呼べる状態となっている。

　屋上に台形の鐘楼を戴き、下部には地下礼拝堂の膨らみを見せる北面。東面は3階が玄関階。4、5階は階高の低い僧房部分で、黒い自然石仕上げPCパネルがハーモニカ状になったバルコニーがある。2層の僧房階が回りこみ、その下に階高の高い教室が、足の長いピロティで持ち上げられている南面。階高の高い食堂（2階）と教室群（3階）、その上4、5階に、高さは東面南面と同じでも、間口が相対的にゆったりした寸法に作られた教授神父用個室のハーモニカ状開口のある西面。主要前面道路の裏側に位置するこの西面がしばしば重視されるのは、2、3階の皮膜として作られた「波動リズムガラス面」、「音楽的ガラス面」と呼ばれる「1/fゆらぎ」のようなランダムなピッチで設けられた細いPCコンクリートの方立てによる床から天井までの大きなガラス面の印象が強いからだ。

　方立てのピッチは、「モデュロール」を用いて決められた。この現場の担当者としてコルビュジェに起用されたのは、ルーマニア生まれのギリシア系仏人スタッフ、イアニス・クセナキス。音楽と建築の両方の才能によるひらめきの成果であった。

　クセナキスは1922年生まれ、今日では、コルビュジェのスタッフであったことはあまり知られていないが、作曲に数学的アプローチを取り入れた前衛音楽家として世界中に知られている（音楽家としては日本語表記で「ヤニス・クセナキス」とされることが多い）。

　コルビュジェの事務所に入った際の彼の立場は、数学と建築を学んだキャリアから、構造エンジニアとしてであった。セルジオ・フェロ他の共著『ル・コルビュジェ、ラ・トゥーレット修道院』（青山マミ訳、TOTO出版）の序文に寄せた彼自身の文章には、「私は当時、チームで唯一の技術担当者」「計算ができるのは私だけだった」と自信のほどが語られている。プロジェクトの進行過程で大いなる変化も生じてくる。「コルビュジェに助けられて

● 波動リズムガラス面
西面からの外観。

undulatory-rhythm glass walls west appearance

Xenakis as a Musician and Structural Engineer

You can walk up a path from the north-east to the Monastery, with a 70ha area on a rolling hill. Though the main frontal road is running the eastside, the building is surrounded by the roads and spacey "panoramic" scenery. Therefore, all the four sides could be called the "frontage".

The north façade has a triangular bell tower on top of the swell of the underground chapel. The east face has an entrance on the 2nd floor and there is a long strip of PC panels of natural black stone finish on the 3rd and 4th floors. These panels are for monk's sleeping cells and are of short floor-to-floor distance. These two layers of monk cells run round to the south side above classrooms. The floor height of the classroom is high and the room is supported by long pilotis. The west façade includes a refectory (dining room) that has a long floor-to-floor distance (1st floor) and classrooms (2nd floor). Upon these, there are harmonica-looking openings of cells for priests, which have the same floor height and a longer frontage compared to the cells for monks of the east and south sides. The west façade is often highlighted, though located behind the east main frontal road, because the glazed walls enveloping the 3rd and 4th floors are highly impressive. They are called "undulatory-rhythm glass walls (ondulatoire)" or "panes of musical glass (pans de verre musicaux)" and reaching from the floor to the ceiling with randomly detailed pitches like a "1/f fluctuation".

These mullions are determined with the Modulor. Le Corbusier used Iannis Xenakis, a Romania-born Greek-French staff, for this site. These impressive walls were a result of flashes of talent both in music and architecture.

Xenakis was born in 1922. He is today known worldwide as an avant-garde musician, but not so much as a staff of Le Corbusier. (His name is written differently in Japanese as a musician from as an architect.)

Xenakis joined the office of Le Corbusier as a structural engineer, who had studied math and architecture. He proudly wrote in a publication that he was the only one to do the math at the team then. He also illustrated that he was the sole staff in charge of engineering ("Le Corbusier, The Monastery of La Tourette", translated by Mami Aoyama, Bookshop TOTO). As the project went on, there was another sea change. Xenakis also indicated that he became involved in architecture through drawing the plans of the Monastery of La Tourette with Le Corbusier's help.

Later on, there was also a pleasant surprise for the architect, who used him. That is, integration of music and architecture, Xenakis' long-time conceptual or abstract theme, was experimented and

ラ・トゥーレット修道院の図面を描くことで、技術者だった私は建築にのめり込んでいった」（同）。

やがて彼を起用した建築家にも予想外の良循環が発生する。「長いこと私が（コンセプトとして）つまり抽象的には追求していたテーマである音楽と建築の関係、その統合が実験され具体化されていった」（同）。

修道院の西面のファサードの過半、中庭の十字形通路の大半を占め、建物の表情の多くを決定づけることになる「オンデュラトワール」はこうして誕生した。

居心地のよい修道僧の個室

4、5階にある修道僧用個室と教授用個室は、中庭側の2.26m×2.26mの断面の廊下から5.92mという共通の奥行きをもって修道僧用が幅1.83m、教授神父用が幅2.26m（寸法はすべてモデュロールに準拠）となってコの字型の外部に向かって展開し、外周側にバルコニーをもつ。個室内には洗面器のみで、トイレとシャワーはフロアで共用である。

幅1.83mの修道僧用の個室は、現在は訪問者用に解放され、夕食、朝食、昼食までついたフル・ボードの均一宿泊費が45ユーロ。

修道院内では普段と同じ音量での会話が禁止され、ひそひそ話での会話が要求される。両手を伸ばして壁から壁にほぼ届く羊羹のようなプロポーションの個室群。

個室の居住性に関しては決して期待していなかった。しかし、部屋にトイレがないことをのぞけば、思いのほか快適であった。写真家はこの空間が思いのほかお気にいりの様子で「連泊でも、ここにしばらく住んでもいい」と語っていたのが印象深い。

修道僧の個室内部。
inside the cells for monks

realised.

This is how the "ondulatoire" was created, which set the tone for more than half of the west façade and the cross alley of the garden court.

Cozy Cells for Monks

Cells for monks and priests were located towards the outside on the 3rd and 4th floors. They have the same depth of 5.92m from the hallway (1.83m for rooms for monks and 2.26m for priests according to the Modulor) with balconies on the outer side. The section of the corridor at the garden court is 2.26m×2.26m. Each cell has only a basin and there are common cloakrooms and shower rooms for each floor.

Overnight stays in the unused cells with full board can be now arranged for visitors for €45.

It is prohibited to speak at a normal volume and you should talk in whispers. Units are a rectangular solid shape in which you can almost touch both the walls.

I had not expected much for the interior comfort of the cells. But, it was astonishingly livable except there was no cloakroom in the cell. The photographer looked pleased enough by the room to say "I can stay here for some nights or even live for a while." It was impressive.

「修道院」像の大いなる振幅

カトリックv.s.プロテスタント

　キリスト教会では聖職者（僧侶）の呼称が明確に異なる。カトリック教会には「牧師」は一人もいない。カトリック教会にいる聖職者は「神父」である。結婚式でバージンロードを、祭壇に向かって、父親が花嫁と一緒に歩くのはプロテスタント。新郎が花嫁と歩くのがカトリックだ。

　「宗教なんかあるから平和にならない（『Imagine』の歌詞）」と、かつてジョン・レノンが喝破した。宗教が、もし本当に人々を救済するものであるのなら、古来、イスラム教徒とキリスト教徒が延々と血みどろの殺戮を繰り返してきたことをどう説明するのか？さらにキリスト教社会の内部でも、16世紀後半のパリではカトリックの民衆がプロテスタントを襲い、2千〜3千人を殺した（『聖バルテルミーの虐殺』）、この手の凄惨な事件をどう説明するのか？

　話を戻そう。修道院という若い聖職者のための修練道場の仕組みがあるのはカトリック教会（もしくはギリシア正教会）であり、歴史上、1〜2の例外を除き、プロテスタントの教会には修道院は存在しない。

カトリックと修道院の歴史

　「修道院長」という役職は、修道院の創成期には謹厳実直にして「勤勉、質素、服従」「禁欲、清貧、貞潔」といった教義を忠実に守り、若い修行僧のトレーニングの指導者としてふさわしい人格者であったはずである。しかしながら、歴史上、修道院長は、そのイメージの振幅が非常に大きい。

　修道院長に止まらず、司祭→司教→枢機卿→教皇というカトリックの権力構造のヒエラルキーの中で、時代により、それぞれの役職イメージの「善と悪」「聖と俗」のコントラストが非常に強いという共通点がある。地上における『神の代理人』とされる「ローマ法王」職でも、考えられないようなワル、大俗人など明らかな不適格者の存在が歴史に記録されている。

　普段の戒律や行動規範が厳しいために、ひとたびその束縛を解かれた時に、反動で「地が出る」ことになり物議をかもす。世間の顰蹙を買うという点で、「教師と坊主は助平」という世界共通の現象が観察されることが少なくない。

起源

　修道院という若い宗教者の訓練機関の起源は、西暦529年頃、ローマの南にあるモンテ・カシノに聖ベネディクトゥス（480〜550頃）が修道院を開いたことによる。学問研究から農業や他のあらゆる産業の基本的な枠組みをつくるのに寄与したとされる初期の修道士を多数指導した『聖ベネディクトゥス戒律』は、その後のカトリック世界の指導原理となった。

　しかしながら、ヨーロッパ中世初期は国家の輪郭があいまいな流動期であり、10世紀から11世紀前半まで、俗人貴族が建立した私立の教会や修道院もでき、妻子や兵士を抱える俗人修道院長も存在したことが記録されている。

クリュニー会

　修道院の歴史の第一次改革期とでも言うべき流れが、フランス、ブルゴーニュ地方南部、マコンの北西20km（リヨンの北約80km）にあるクリュニーに起こる。『聖ベネディクトゥス戒律』の基本を改めて尊重するクリュニー修道院は、11世紀の前半に創立され、その後の約200年間に傑出した修道院長が代々続き、ヨーロッパ各地の1500を越える修道院からなる巨大な修道院連合を組織するに至る。聖職の売買（俗人の修道院長任命など）や聖職者

の結婚の禁止など、修道院の基本の徹底が図られる。

シトー会

僧衣の色から「黒い修道士」の異名を持つクリュニー会の修道士に対し、白い未晒しの衣服を着る習慣によって「白い修道士」と呼ばれるのが、11世紀末期にクリュニー会から分離したシトー会である。クリュニー会がめざしたところが『聖ベネディクトゥス戒律』の精神に戻ることではあったものの、修道院連合が巨大化すると共に、財政規模が膨らみ、修道士の他に、助修士、俗人雇用者なども抱え、意に反して俗事に煩わされることが多くなる。シトー会の設立に動いたモレームのロベルトゥスは、奢侈傾向の見られるクリュニー会を嫌い、ディジョンの南23km（クリュニーの北80km）の広漠とした森林の広がるシトーに修道院を築き、修道士だけですべてを賄い、俗世間と離れて神への奉仕にのみ捧げる生活を始める。

13世紀に入ると、スペイン、バレンシアの聖ドミニクス（1170～1221）を創始者とするドミニコ修道会、イタリア、アッシジの聖フランチェスコ（1181～1226）を開祖とするフランチェスコ（フランシスコ）修道会が修道院の世俗化に対する改革運動に合流する。

ル・トロネ修道院

歴史の記述が長くなったが、ラ・トゥーレット修道院を語る際に欠かせない、プロバンスのル・トロネ修道院（エクス・アン・プロバンスの東約65km）の記述をするためにも、その背景説明が必要であった。

ラ・トゥーレット修道院の勧進元（発注者）の代表者である神父マリー・アラン・クテュリエが、設計者に決まったル・コルビュジェに、見に行くように指示したのがシトー会のル・トロネ修道院であった。ラ・トゥーレット修道院のデザインが、ル・トロネ修道院からの影響下（コルビュジェは何度も訪れ、実測もしたと伝えられる）でまとめられたという以上に、ル・トロネの「生まれ変わり」に近いものが感じられる。現代建築でありつつ、歴史的な宗教者の精神の営みを踏まえ、それに建築家自身のイメージの羽をつけて展開したという経過により、ラ・トゥーレットは格別な存在となった。

クテュリエ神父が「典型的なシトー会修道院を見てきてくれ」と伝えた背景の解明には、修道院史のさらに続きが必要である。

ちなみに、ラ・トゥーレット修道院はシトー会ではなく、ドミニク会の修道院である。

ル・トロネ修道院　撮影：笠原一人©

聖と俗のスパイラル

　カトリック教会（修道院）の俗化・堕落・腐敗と、それに対する反発・反省・改革のスパイラルは、クリュニー会やシトー会等の発足以降も、実は延々と繰り返される。

　塩野七生の『神の代理人』『チェーザレ・ボルジアあるいは優雅なる冷酷』などに詳しい記述があるが、法王職は、コンクラーベ（法王選出会議）によって、健康に不安のある高齢の枢機卿を法王に選ぶことはないはずであるが、歴史上73年間に24名の法王が交代した時期がある。天命を全うしての死は少なく、虚々実々の陰謀渦巻く権力闘争の結果として「他殺」説も有力である。

　16世紀にはいると、「免罪符」の販売で教会が腐敗の極に達した状況下、マルチン・ルターがウイッテンベルクで宗教改革の狼煙（のろし）を上げる。宗教改革の流れは国際的なものとなり、この時点でカトリック勢力は「初心」を改めて思い出すことになる。

　先のシトー会の改革が第二次改革期と数えるならドイツのルター、スイスのカルバンらの改革は第三次改革期と言える。

イエズス会

　ルターらプロテスタントの改革運動が大いなる刺激となって、いわば外圧による改革ではなく、カトリック内部での自主変革を目指すというのが「反宗教改革」または「対抗宗教改革」と呼ばれる。これが数えて第四次の改革期である。

　イグナチオ・デ・ロヨラ（1491〜1556）を代表としフランシスコ・ザビエル（1506〜52）らと結成したイエズス会がその中心となった。大学や大きな図書館をつくり、対抗宗教改革のための陣容の建直しが行われた。

シトー会の衰退とクリュニー会系の豪華修道院のゆくえ

　様々な勢力の栄枯盛衰は世の常であるが、修道院の原点に戻り、修道士のみの自給自足の中での修行を徹底するというシトー会の勢力は、多数派になることはなく、15世紀から早くも凋落の道をたどる。18世紀になると修道士がついにいなくなる。

　その一方で『聖ベネディクトゥス戒律』を基本としながらもクリュニー会では、聖堂を飾るための芸術、装飾には莫大な金を惜しげもなく投入した。主を賛美するためには、祈りは当然であるが、さらに「美を奉納する」という趣旨で、全能の神の栄光を信者の誰にも容易に理解させるため、教会の内外の細部に至るまで装飾を施すこととなった。

　経済の急成長状況下、王や貴族の懐も潤い、権勢の表現手段としてのバロック芸術、さら

クリュニー修道院　撮影：奥佳弥©

セナンク修道院　撮影：中村大吾©

にそれが進んで生まれた支流たるロココ様式も本格化する。

まさにこの流れは、教会を飾りたてたいクリュニー会（多くは「ベネディクト修道院」を名乗っているが）の思惑に一致して今日も残る修道院建築、メルク修道院（オーストリア、世界遺産）、ザンクトガレン修道院（スイス、同）、クレメンティヌムの修道院（チェコ、同）、ストラホフ修道院（チェコ、同）、といった突き抜けた超豪華修道院となる。

修道院の歴史において奢侈志向は繰り返し反省材料となったにもかかわらず、古今東西いつの時代にもある「喉元過ぎて、熱さを忘れる」人間の本性で、「美の奉納」と「美の放蕩」の区別がつかなくなる。18世紀というのは、歴史上、世の中がもっともおおっぴらにエロチックであった時代であった。そんな社会にあって、修道院も例外ではなくなり、ついには淫蕩を極めるところまで堕ちる（エードゥアルト・フックス著『風俗の歴史』や福田和彦著『世界性風俗じてん』などには、多くのベネディクト派修道院での院長や僧侶の蓄妾。尼僧院の娼家化と堕胎。嬰児を壁に塗りこんで…という類の話が数多く紹介されている）。

以上は、勧進元であるクテュリエ神父が、ラ・トゥーレット修道院の建設に際し、追求した修道院像のバックグラウンドを、できるだけ時系列に沿ってまとめたものである。

4つのシトー会修道院に倣う

ラ・トゥーレット修道院のデザイン規範となったシトー会のル・トロネ修道院（1190年竣工）には、実は「姉妹」がいる。「プロヴァンス地方の三姉妹」と並び称されるあとふたつのシトー会の修道院が、セナンク修道院（1178年竣工）とシルヴァカンヌ修道院（1230年竣工）である。さらに、少し北に離れるが、ブルゴーニュ地方、ディジョンの北約30kmに位置するフォントネー修道院（1140年竣工、世界遺産）を入れて「シトー会の四姉妹」と呼んでも差し支えないと思えるほどに、ロマネスク様式の同時代にあって、それぞれが共通の特徴を備えている。

聖堂を「ロの字型」平面の一辺とする。矩形の中庭を囲む列柱廊。壮麗さを否定した無装飾を基本とする内部外部。

無地の石積みが打ち放しコンクリートに読み替えられているが、これらの特徴はそのままラ・トゥーレット修道院に継承されている。思索と瞑想の場たる回廊（列柱廊）は、800年の時空を経て、「四姉妹」とは造形的には著しい相違点であるが、光と影の織り成す効果を生かすという点において、ラ・トゥーレット修道院では「波動リズムガラス面」（前述）として意訳されたかたちとなった。

シルヴァカンヌ修道院
撮影：中村大吾©

フォントネー修道院　撮影：中村大吾©

宮本和義 ©	Photos	© Kazuyoshi Miyamoto
栗田仁 ©	Text	© Jin Kurita
牧尾晴喜 [スタジオOJMM] ©	Translation	© Haruki Makio [Studio OJMM]
石原秀一	Chief Editor	Shuichi Ishihara
大石雄一朗、戸嶋彩香	Staff Editors	Yuichiro Oishi, Ayaka Toshima
片岡智深		Tomomi Kataoka
馬嶋正司 [(株)ポパイ]	Design	Shoji Majima (Popai, Inc.)
城下実 [(株)あるす]	Printer	Minoru Joshita (ARS CO.,LTD)
松尾茂男	Drafting	Shigeo Matsuo

コルビュジェ財団、朝日新聞社 西村博之、リネア建築企画 笠原一人、奥佳弥 中村大吾、よしだまき （順不同）	Special Thanks	Foundation Le Corbusier, The Asahi Shimbun Company Hiroyuki Nishimura, Linea CO.,LTD Kazuto Kasahara, Kaya Oku Daigo Nakamura, Maki Yoshida

ラ・トゥーレット修道院
1953-1960 フランス
ル・コルビュジェ
2007年4月15日発行

Monastery of Sainte-Marie de La Tourette
1953-1960 France
Le Corbusier
15/4/2007

石原秀一	Publisher	Shuichi Ishihara
バナナブックス ©		© Banana Books
〒151-0051東京都渋谷区千駄ヶ谷5-17-15		5-17-15 Sendagaya Shibuya-ku,Tokyo, 151-0051 Japan
TEL.03-5367-6838 FAX.03-5367-4635		Tel.＋81-3-5367-6838 Fax.+81-3-5367-4635
URL: http://bananabooks.cc/		URL: http://bananabooks.cc/

BANANA BOOKS
PRINTED IN JAPAN
ISBN978-4-902930-10-8 C3352
©FLC/ADAGP,Paris&SPDA,Tokyo,2007

禁無断転載
落丁・乱丁本はおとりかえします。